Becoming Your Own Therapist

MAY THE BUDDHADHARMA REACH ALL SENTIENT BEINGS · LAMA YESHE WISDOM ARCHIVE ·

Previously published by the LAMA YESHE WISDOM ARCHIVE

Becoming Your Own Therapist, by Lama Yeshe
Advice for Monks and Nuns, by Lama Yeshe and Lama Zopa Rinpoche
Virtue and Reality, by Lama Zopa Rinpoche
Make Your Mind an Ocean, by Lama Yeshe

Forthcoming in 1999

Teachings at the Vajrasattva Retreat (February-April, 1999), by Lama
    Zopa Rinpoche
A Chat about Heruka, by Lama Zopa Rinpoche
A Chat about Yamantaka, by Lama Zopa Rinpoche

(contact us for information)

*May whoever sees, touches, reads, remembers, or talks or thinks about these
booklets never be reborn in unfortunate circumstances, receive only
rebirths in situations conducive to the perfect practice of Dharma, meet
only perfecyly qualified spiritual guides, quickly develop bodhicitta and
immediately attain enlightenment for the sake of all sentient beings.*

Lama Yeshe

Becoming Your Own Therapist

An Introduction to the Buddhist Way of Thought

Edited by Nicholas Ribush

Lama Yeshe Wisdom Archive • Boston

A non-profit charitable organization for the benefit of all
sentient beings and a section of the Foundation for the
Preservation of the Mahayana Tradition
www.fpmt.org

First published 1998
10,000 copies for free distribution
Second printing 1998, 12,000
Third printing 1999, 8,000

LAMA YESHE WISDOM ARCHIVE
PO BOX 356
WESTON
MA 02493 USA

ISBN 1-891868-00-4

10 9 8 7 6 5 4 3

Front cover photograph by Ricardo de Aratanha
Back cover photograph by Ueli Minder

Printed in Canada

Please contact the LAMA YESHE WISDOM ARCHIVE for more free
copies of this booklet

Contents

BENEFACTOR'S DEDICATION

In loving memory of my dear parents Glenice and Jack Custy, who were renowned among their friends and associates for their kindness, integrity and wisdom; who gave me a perfect human rebirth with the best education and enjoyments; and who showed me through their example as parents the meaning of self-sacrifice, honesty and unconditional love. In all their future lives, may they only have good health, happiness and ease most quickly perfecting the path to Enlightenment.

Through the clear flawless teachings of my precious spiritual parents Lama Yeshe and Lama Zopa Rinpoche, I have a little understanding of the meaning of mother and father sentient beings' incredible kindness and suffering. May Lama Ösel Rinpoche and Lama Zopa Rinpoche live long healthy lives and all their wishes be fulfilled without hindrance.

—*Ecie Hursthouse*

PUBLISHER'S NOTE

We are extremely grateful to Ecie Hursthouse for sponsoring this reprint of Lama Yeshe's extremely popular *Becoming Your Own Therapist* in memory of her late parents, for their sake and for that of all sentient beings. Recently Lama Zopa Rinpoche explained that sponsoring the publication of Dharma teachings in memory of deceased relatives and friends was very common in Tibet and is of great benefit. Therefore, the LAMA YESHE WISDOM ARCHIVE encourages others who might like to make booklets of teachings by Lama Yeshe and Lama Zopa Rinpoche available for free distribution in this way to contact us for more information. Thank you so much.

EDITOR'S INTRODUCTION

Lama Yeshe's teachings are unique. Nobody taught like Lama. Spontaneous, from the heart, in the moment, direct; every word an instruction to be practiced. Lama's English was unique. Nobody spoke like Lama. Highly creative, Lama expressed himself not only verbally, but physically and facially as well. How to convey this miraculous transmission on paper? As I have noted elsewhere, those of us presented with this challenge do the best we can.

As Lama frequently liked to point out, his teachings were not dry, academic, philosophical discourses but practical, down-to-earth methods for looking within and understanding the mind. Lama always challenged us to find out who we are, what we are. In his inimitable, provocative style, he would dare us to examine our preconceptions fearlessly, in the hope that we would see for ourselves how everything comes from the mind; that we create our own suffering and happiness; that we must take personal responsibility for whatever we experience, good or bad.

In this booklet we offer three talks by Lama Yeshe on the general topic of Buddhism. They were public lectures given more than twenty years ago to mainly Western audiences. Nevertheless, as Lama also liked to point out, Lord Buddha's timeless teachings are as universally relevant today as they were when they were first given, over 2,500 years ago. Therefore, there is no doubt that now, a mere two decades down the road, Lama Yeshe's teachings are as globally applicable as they were back in the seventies.

Each lecture is followed by a question and answer session. Lama and his audiences always enjoyed the give and take of these lively exchanges, and pretty much anything went. For most people, it was their first ever encounter with a Tibetan lama, and they brought along several years' worth of questions. As is apparent, Lama handled everything with great compassion, humor and aplomb.

Although these talks were called lectures, I think Lama would have each of us use them as a mirror for our minds and look beyond the words, find ourselves, and become our own psychologist.

I would like to thank Cheryl Bentsen, Rand Engel and Wendy Cook for their insightful comments, which greatly improved the edited version of these talks, and Garrett Brown and Jennifer Martin for their help in the design and production of this booklet.

Finding Ourselves Through Buddhism

When we study Buddhism, we are studying ourselves, the nature of our own minds. Instead of focusing on some supreme being, Buddhism emphasizes more practical matters, such as how to lead our lives, how to integrate our minds and how to keep our everyday lives peaceful and healthy. In other words, Buddhism always accentuates experiential knowledge-wisdom rather than some dogmatic view. In fact, we don't even consider Buddhism to be a religion in the usual sense of the term. From the lamas' point of view, Buddhist teachings are more in the realm of philosophy, science or psychology.

The human mind instinctively seeks happiness. East, West—there's no difference; everybody's doing the same thing. But if your search for happiness is causing you to grasp emotionally at the sense world, it can be very dangerous. You have no control.

Now, don't think that control is an Eastern thing, a Buddhist thing. We all need control, especially those of us caught up in the materialistic life; psychologically, emotionally, we're too involved in objects of attachment. From the Buddhist point of view, that's an unhealthy mind; the person is mentally ill.

Actually, you already know that external, scientific technological development alone cannot satisfy the desires of your attachment or solve your other emotional problems. But what Lord Buddha's teaching shows you is the characteristic nature of human potential, the capacity of the human mind. When you study Buddhism, you learn what you are and how to develop further; instead of emphasizing some kind of supernatural belief system, Buddhist methods teach you to develop a deep understanding of yourself and all other phenomena.

However, whether you are religious or a ⌐
believer or an atheist, it is crucial that you know h
mind works. If you don't, you'll go around thi
healthy, when in reality, the deep root of afflictive ⌐
true cause of all psychological disease, is there, gr⌐
you. Because of that, all it takes is some tiny e⌐
changing, something insignificant going wrong, ⌐
few seconds, you're completely upset. To me, that ⌐
mentally ill. Why? Because you're obsessed wit
world, blinded by attachment, and under the co
fundamental cause of all problems, not knowing t
your own mind.

It doesn't matter if you try to refute what I'n
telling me that you don't believe it. It's not a questi
No matter how much you say, "I don't believe I h⌐
your nose is still there, right between your eyes. Y
always there, whether you believe it or not.

I've met many people who proudly proclaim, "I'm not a
believer." They're so proud of their professed lack of belief in
anything. You check up; this is important to know. In the world
today there are so many contradictions. Scientific materialists
boast, "I don't believe"; religious people say, "I believe." But no
matter what you think, you still need to know the characteristic
nature of your own mind. If you don't, then no matter how
much you talk about the shortcomings of attachment, you have
no idea what attachment actually is or how to control it. Words
are easy. What's really difficult is to understand the true nature
of attachment.

For example, when people first made cars and planes, their
intention was to be able to do things more quickly so that
they'd have more time for rest. But what's happened instead is
that people are more restless than ever. Examine your own
everyday life. Because of attachment, you get emotionally
involved in a concrete sense world of your own creation,
denying yourself the space or time to see the reality of your
own mind. To me, that's the very definition of a difficult life.
You cannot find satisfaction or enjoyment. The truth is that
pleasure and joy actually come from the mind, not from
objective phenomena.

Nevertheless, some intelligent, skeptical people do
understand to a degree that material objects do not guarantee a

worthwhile, enjoyable life and are trying to see if there really is something else that might offer true satisfaction.

When Lord Buddha spoke about suffering, he wasn't referring simply to superficial problems like illness and injury, but to the fact that the dissatisfied nature of the mind itself is suffering. No matter how much of something you get, it never satisfies your desire for better or more. This unceasing desire is suffering; its nature is emotional frustration.

Buddhist psychology describes six basic emotions that frustrate the human mind, disturbing its peace, making it restless: ignorance, attachment, anger, pride, deluded doubt and distorted views. These are mental attitudes, not external phenomena. Buddhism emphasizes that to overcome these delusions, the root of all your suffering, belief and faith are not much help: you have to understand their nature.

If you do not investigate your own mind with introspective knowledge-wisdom, you will never see what's in there. Without checking, no matter how much you talk about your mind and your emotions, you'll never really understand that your basic emotion is egocentricity and that this is what's making you restless.

Now, to overcome your ego you don't have to give up all your possessions. Keep your possessions; they're not what's making your life difficult. You're restless because you are clinging to your possessions with attachment; ego and attachment pollute your mind, making it unclear, ignorant and agitated, and prevent the light of wisdom from growing. The solution to this problem is meditation.

Meditation does not imply only the development of single pointed concentration, sitting in some corner doing nothing. Meditation is an alert state of mind, the opposite of sluggishness; meditation is wisdom. You should remain aware every moment of your daily life, fully conscious of what you are doing and why and how you are doing it.

We do almost everything unconsciously. We eat unconsciously; we drink unconsciously; we talk unconsciously. Although we claim to be conscious, we are completely unaware of the afflictions rampaging through our minds, influencing everything we do.

Check up for yourselves; experiment. I'm not being judgmental or putting you down. This is how Buddhism works. It gives you ideas that you can check out in your own experience to see if they're true or not. It's very down-to-earth; I'm not talking about something way up there in the sky. It's actually a very simple thing.

If you don't know the characteristic nature of attachment and its objects, how can you generate loving kindness towards your friends, your parents or your country? From the Buddhist point of view, it's impossible. When you hurt your parents or your friends, it's your unconscious mind at work. When acting out his anger, the angry person is completely oblivious as to what's happening in his mind. Being unconscious makes us hurt and disrespect other sentient beings; being unaware of our own behavior and mental attitude makes us lose our humanity. That's all. It's so simple, isn't it?

These days, people study and train to become psychologists. Lord Buddha's idea is that everybody should become a psychologist. Each of us should know our own mind; you should become your own psychologist. This is definitely possible; every human being has the ability to understand his or her own mind. When you understand your own mind, control follows naturally.

Don't think that control is just some Himalayan trip or that it must be easier for people who don't have many possessions. That's not necessarily true. Next time you are emotionally upset, check for yourself. Instead of busily doing something to distract yourself, relax and try to become aware of what you're doing. Ask yourself, "Why am I doing this? How am I doing it? What's the cause?" You will find this to be a wonderful experience. Your main problem is a lack of intensive knowledge-wisdom, awareness, or consciousness. Therefore, you will discover that through understanding, you can easily solve your problems.

To feel loving kindness for others, you have to know the nature of the object. If you don't, then even though you say, "I love him; I love her," it's just your arrogant mind taking you on yet another ego trip. Make sure you know how and why. It is very important that you become your own psychologist. Then you can treat yourself through the understanding wisdom of your own mind; you'll be able to relax with and enjoy your friends and possessions instead of becoming restless and berserk and wasting your life.

To become your own psychologist, you don't have to learn some big philosophy. All you have to do is examine your own mind every day. You already examine material things every day—every morning you check out the food in your kitchen—but you never investigate your mind. Checking your mind is much more important.

Nevertheless, most people seem to believe the opposite. They seem to think that they can simply buy the solution to whatever problem they're facing. The materialistic attitude that money can buy whatever you need to be happy, that you can purchase a peaceful mind, is obviously not true, but even though you may not say the words, this is what you're thinking. It's a complete misconception.

Even people who consider themselves religious need to understand their own minds. Faith alone never stops problems; understanding knowledge-wisdom always does. Lord Buddha himself said that belief in Buddha was dangerous; that instead of just believing in something, people should use their minds to try to discover their own true nature. Belief based on understanding is fine; once you realize or are intellectually clear about something, belief follows automatically. However, if your faith is based on misconceptions it can easily be destroyed by what others say.

Unfortunately, even though they consider themselves religious, many spiritually inclined people are weak. Why? Because they don't understand the true nature of their mind. If you really know what your mind is and how it works, you'll understand that it's mental energy that prevents you from being healthy. When you understand your own mind's view, or perception, of the world, you'll realize that not only are you constantly grasping at the sense world, but also that what you're grasping at is merely imaginary. You will see that you're too concerned with what's going to happen in a non-existent future and totally unconscious of the present moment, that you are living for a mere projection. Don't you agree that a mind that is unconscious in the present and constantly grasping at the future is unhealthy?

It is important to be conscious in your everyday life. The nature of conscious awareness and wisdom is peace and joy. You don't need to grasp at some future resultant joy. As long as you follow the path of right understanding and right action to the best of your ability, the result will be immediate, simultaneous with the action. You don't have to think, "If I spend my lifetime acting right, perhaps I'll get some good result in my next life." You don't need to obsess over the attainment of future realizations. As long as you act in the present with as much understanding as you possibly can, you'll realize everlasting peace in no time at all.

And I think that's enough from me. Better that we have a question and answer session, instead of my talking all the time. Thank you.

Q. When you were talking about meditation, you didn't mention visualization. It seems that some people find it relatively easy to visualize while others find it quite difficult. How important is it to develop the ability to visualize things in the mind?

Lama. Many people have trouble visualizing what's described to them simply because they have not trained their minds in it, but for others it's because they have a poor imagination; they're too physical. Perhaps they think that all there is to their being is their physical body, that there's no mind apart from their brain. However, Buddhism has methods whereby you can train your mind and develop the ability to visualize in meditation. But in reality, you visualize all day long. The breakfast you eat in the morning is a visualization. Whenever you go shopping and think, "This is nice," or "I don't like that," whatever you're looking at is a projection of your own mind. When you get up in the morning and see the sun shining and think, "Oh, it's going to be nice today," that's your own mind visualizing. Actually, visualization is quite well understood. Even shopkeepers and advertising agents know the importance of visualization, so they create displays or billboards to attract your attention: "Buy this!" They know that things you see affect your mind, your visualization. Visualization is not something supernatural; it's scientific.

Q. From what you say, I get the impression you're somewhat critical of the West, that you laugh at what we do and the way we try to civilize the uncivilized. I don't really have a question, but what future do you see for mankind in terms of what the so-called progressive West is developing: bigger planes, bigger houses, bigger supermarkets? What future do you see for the West?

Lama. I see that Western people are getting busier and busier, more and more restless. I'm not criticizing material or technological development as such, but rather the uncontrolled mind. Because you don't know who or what you are, you spend your life blindly grasping at what I call "supermarket goodness." You agitate your own life; you make yourself restless. Instead of integrating your life, you splinter it. Check up for yourself. I'm not putting you down. In fact, Buddhism doesn't allow us to dogmatically put down anybody else's way of life. All I'm trying to suggest is that you consider looking at things another way.

Q. Lama, like yourself, most of the Tibetan teachers we see are men. I was wondering if there are any female *rinpoches* or *tulkus*?
Lama. Yes, of course. Men and women are completely equal when it comes to developing higher states of mind. In Tibet, monks would sometimes take teachings from female rinpoches. Buddhism teaches that you can't judge people from the outside; you can't say, "He's nothing; I'm special." You can never really tell by outer appearances who's higher and who's lower.

Q. Is the role of a Buddhist nun very different from that of a monk?
Lama. Not really. They study the same things and teach their students in the same way.

Q. Sometimes it's hard to find a teacher. Is it dangerous to try to practice tantra, for example, without a teacher, just by reading books?
Lama. Yes, very dangerous. Without specific instructions, you can't just pick up a book on tantra and think, "Wow, what fantastic ideas. I want to practice this right now!" This kind of attitude never brings realizations. You need the guidance of an experienced teacher. Sure, the ideas are fantastic, but if you don't know the method, you can't put them into your own experience; you have to have the key. Many Buddhist books have been translated into English. They'll tell you, "Attachment is bad; don't get angry," but how do you actually abandon attachment and anger? The Bible, too, recommends

universal love, but how do you bring universal love into your own experience? You need the key, and sometimes only a teacher can give you that.

Q. What should people in the West do when they can't find a teacher? Should those who are really searching go to the East to find one?
Lama. Don't worry. When the time is right, you'll meet your teacher. Buddhism doesn't believe that you can push other people: "Everybody should learn to meditate; everybody should become Buddhists." That's stupid. Pushing people is unwise. When you're ready, some kind of magnetic energy will bring you together with your teacher. About going to the East, it depends on your personal situation. Check up. The important thing is to search with wisdom and not blind faith. Sometimes, even if you go to the East, you still can't find a teacher. It takes time.

Q. What is the Buddhist attitude towards suicide?
Lama. People who take their own lives have no understanding of the purpose or value of being born human. They kill themselves out of ignorance. They can't find satisfaction, so they think, "I'm hopeless."

Q. If a person, out of ignorance perhaps, believes he has achieved enlightenment, what is his purpose in continuing to live?
Lama. An ignorant person who thinks he's enlightened is completely mentally polluted and is simply compounding the ignorance he already has. All he has to do is to check the actions of his uncontrolled mind and he'll realize he's not enlightened. Also, you don't have to ask others, "Am I enlightened?" Just check your own experiences. Enlightenment is a highly personal thing.

Q. I like the way that you stress the importance of understanding over belief, but I find it difficult to know how a person brought up in the West or given a scientific education can understand the concept of reincarnation: past, present and future lives. How can you prove that they exist?
Lama. If you can realize your own mind's continuity from the time you were a tiny embryo in your mother's womb up to the present time, then you'll understand. The continuity of

your mental energy is a bit like the flow of electricity from a generator through the wires until it lights up a lamp. From the moment it's conceived, as your body evolves, mental energy is constantly running through it—changing, changing, changing—and if you can realize that, you can more easily understand your own mind's *previous* continuity. As I keep saying, it's never simply a question of *belief*. Of course, initially it's difficult to accept the idea of reincarnation because these days it's such a new concept for most people, especially those brought up in the West. They don't teach you continuity of consciousness in school; you don't study the nature of the mind—who you are, what you are—in college. So of course, it's all new to you. But if you think it's important to know who and what you are, and you investigate your mind through meditation, you will easily come to understand the difference between your body and your mind; you will recognize the continuity of your own consciousness; from there you will be able to realize your previous lives. It is not necessary to accept reincarnation on faith alone.

Q. Could you please explain the relationship between meditation, enlightenment and supernormal mental powers, such as seeing the future, reading other people's minds and seeing what's happening in a place that's far away?
Lama. While it's definitely possible to achieve clairvoyance through developing single-pointed concentration, we have a long way to go. As you slowly, slowly gain a better understanding of your own mind, you will gradually develop the ability to see such things. But it's not that easy, where you meditate just once and all of a sudden you can see the future or become enlightened. It takes time.

Q. If you are meditating, working towards enlightenment, do these powers come with control or just all of a sudden, with no control at all?
Lama. True powers come with control. They're not like the uncontrolled emotional hallucinations you experience after you've taken drugs. Even before you reach enlightenment, you can develop insight into your past and future lives and read other people's minds, but this comes about only through the controlled and gradual development of wisdom.

Q. Do you yourself have the power to separate your mind from your body and astral travel or do other things?
Lama. No.

Q. Does His Holiness the Dalai Lama have the power to do that?
Lama. The Mahayana Buddhism of Tibet certainly does contain an unbroken oral tradition of teachings on the development of supernormal powers, which has passed from realized guru to disciple from the time of the Buddha himself down to the present, but even though that teaching exists, it doesn't mean that I have accomplished it. Furthermore, Tibetan Buddhism prohibits any lama who does have such realizations from proclaiming them. Even when you do attain enlightenment, unless there's a good reason, you're not allowed to go around telling everyone that you're a buddha. Be careful. Our system is different from yours. In the West, you hear of people who say, "Last night God spoke to me in my dreams." We think it can be dangerous for people to broadcast details of their mystical experiences, therefore, we don't allow it.

Q. Some years ago I read a book called *The Third Eye* about a gentleman who had extraordinary powers. Have many people had their third eye opened?
Lama. What the author of that book, Lobsang Rampa, says is a literal misconception. The third eye is not a physical thing but rather a metaphor for wisdom. Your third eye is the one that sees beyond ordinary sense perception into the nature of your own mind.

Q. Since Buddhism believes in reincarnation, can you tell me how long there is between lives?
Lama. It can be anything from a few moments up to seven weeks. At the moment the consciousness separates from the body, the subtle body of the intermediate state is already there, waiting for it. Due to the force of craving for another physical body, the intermediate state being searches for an appropriate form, and when it finds one, it takes rebirth.

Q. How does Buddhism explain the population explosion? If you believe in reincarnation, how is it that the population is expanding all the time?

Lama. That's simple. Like modern science, Buddhism talks about the existence of billions and billions of galaxies. The consciousness of a person born on earth may have come from a galaxy far away, drawn here by the force of karma, which connects that person's mental energy to this planet. On the other hand, the consciousness of a person dying on this earth may at the time of death be karmically directed to a rebirth in another galaxy, far from here. If more minds are being drawn to earth, the population increases; if fewer, it declines. That does not mean that brand new minds are coming into existence. Each mind taking rebirth here on earth has come from its previous life—perhaps in another galaxy, perhaps on earth itself, but not from nowhere—in accordance with the cyclic nature of worldly existence.

Q. Is Buddhist meditation better than any other form of meditation or is it simply a case of different forms of meditation suiting different people?
Lama. I can't say that Buddhist meditation is better than that of other religions. It all depends upon the individual.

Q. If someone were already practicing one form of meditation, say, transcendental meditation, would there be any point in that person trying Buddhist meditation as well?
Lama. Not necessarily. If you find that your meditation practice completely awakens your mind and brings you everlasting peace and satisfaction, why try anything else? But if, despite your practice, your mind remains polluted and your actions are still uncontrolled—constantly, instinctively giving harm to others—I think you have a long way to go, baby. It's a very personal thing.

Q. Can a bodhisattva be a Marxist in order to create social harmony? I mean, is there a place for the bodhisattva in Marxism or, *vice versa*, is there a place in Marxism for the bodhisattva? Could Marxism be a tool in the abolition of all sentient beings' suffering?
Lama. Well, it's pretty hard for someone like me to comment on a bodhisattva's actions, but I have my doubts about a bodhisattva becoming a communist in order to stop social problems. Problems exist in the minds of individuals. *You* have

to solve your *own* problems, no matter what kind of society you live in, socialist, communist or capitalist. You must check your own mind. Your problem is not society's problem, not my problem. You are responsible for your own problems just as you're responsible for your own liberation or enlightenment. Otherwise you're going to say, "Supermarkets help people because they can buy the stuff they need in them. If I work in a supermarket I'll really be contributing to society." Then, after doing that for a while, you're going to say, "Maybe supermarkets don't help that much after all. I'd be of more help to others if I took a job in an office." None of those things solve social problems. But first of all you have to check where you got the idea that by becoming a communist, a bodhisattva could help all mother sentient beings.

Q. I was thinking that many people in the world today are hungry and deprived of basic needs and that while they're preoccupied with hunger and the safety and security of their family, it's hard for them to grasp the more subtle aspects of phenomena, such as the nature of their own minds.
Lama. Yes, I understand what you are saying. But don't forget that the starving person preoccupied by hunger and the obese person obsessing over what else to buy in the supermarket are basically the same. Don't just focus on those who are materially deprived. Mentally, rich and poor are equally disturbed, and, fundamentally, one is as unhappy as the other.

Q. But Lord Krishna united India in a spiritual war, the war of Dharma, and as a result, at one time, all the people of India had the ability to engage in spiritual practice. Couldn't we now spread the Dharma amongst all the people on earth and establish a better global society through a kind of spiritual socialism?
Lama. First of all, I think that what you're saying is potentially very dangerous. Only a few people would understand what you're talking about. Generally, you can't say that actions that give harm to mother sentient beings are those of a bodhisattva. Buddhism forbids you to kill other sentient beings, even for supposedly religious reasons. In Buddhism, there's no such thing as a holy war. You have to understand this. And secondly, it's impossible to equalize everybody on earth through force.

Until you fully understand the minds of all beings throughout the universe and have abandoned the minds of self-cherishing and attachment, you will never make all living beings one. It's impossible.

Q. I don't mean making all people the same, because obviously there are going to be different mental levels. But we could establish a universal human society on the basis of socialistic economic theory.

Lama. I think you shouldn't worry about that. You'd be better off worrying about the society of your own mind. That's more worthwhile, more realistic than making projections about what's happening in the world around you.

Q. But is it not a spiritual practice to strike a balance between your own self-realization and service to humanity?

Lama. Yes, you can serve society, but you can't homogenize all sentient beings' actions simultaneously, just like that. Lord Buddha wants all sentient beings to become enlightened right away, but our negative karma is too strong, so we remain uncontrolled. You can't wave a magic wand, "I want everybody to be equally happy," and expect it to happen just like that. Be wise. Only a wise mind can offer equality and peace. You can't do it through emotional rationalization. And you have to know that communist ideas about how best to equalize sentient beings are very different from those of Lord Buddha. You can't mix such different ideas. Don't fantasize; be realistic.

Q. In conclusion, then, are you saying that it's impossible to create one common spiritual society on this planet?

Lama. Even if you could, it would not stop people's problems. Even if you made a single society of all the inhabitants of the entire universe, there would still be attachment, there would still be anger, there would still be hunger. Problems lie within each individual. People are not the same; everybody is different. Each of us needs different methods according to our individual psychological makeup, mental attitudes and personality; each of us needs a different approach in order to attain enlightenment. That's why Buddhism completely accepts the existence of other religions and philosophies. We recognize that they are all necessary for human development. You can't say that any one way of thinking is right for everybody. That's just dogma.

Q. What do you say about drugs that expand the consciousness? Can one experience the bardo under the influence of drugs?
Lama. Yes, it's possible—take an overdose and soon enough you'll experience the bardo. No, I'm just joking. There's no way to get the bardo experience through taking drugs.

Q. Can you read people's auras?
Lama. No, but everybody does have an aura. Aura means vibration. Each of us has our own mental and physical vibration. When you are psychologically upset, your physical environment changes visibly. Everybody goes through that. As science and Buddhism both assert, all physical matter has its own vibration. So people's mental states affect that vibration of their body, and these changes are reflected in the person's aura. That's the simple explanation of the aura. To gain a deep understanding, you have to understand your mind. First learn to read your own mind, then you'll be able to read the minds of others.

Q. How does meditation remove emotional blockages?
Lama. There are many different ways. One is through understanding the nature of your emotions. That way, your emotion is digested into knowledge-wisdom. Digesting your emotions by wisdom is really worthwhile.

Thank you. Good night. Thank you so much.

Auckland, New Zealand
7 June 1975

22

Religion: The Path of Inquiry

People have many different ideas about the nature of religion in general and Buddhism in particular. Those who consider religion and Buddhism at only the superficial, intellectual level will never understand the true significance of either. And those whose view of religion is even more superficial than that will not even consider Buddhism to be a religion at all.

First of all, in Buddhism we're not that interested in talking about the Buddha himself. Nor was he; he wasn't interested in people believing in him, so to this day Buddhism has never encouraged its followers simply to believe in the Buddha. We have always been more interested in understanding human psychology, the nature of the mind. Thus, Buddhist practitioners always try to understand their own mental attitudes, concepts, perceptions and consciousness. Those are the things that really matter.

Otherwise, if you forget about yourself and your delusions and focus instead on some lofty idea—like "What is Buddha?"—your spiritual journey becomes a dream-like hallucination. That's possible; be careful. In your mind there's no connection between Buddha, or God, and yourself. They're completely separate things: you're completely down here; Buddha, or God, is completely up there. There's no connection whatsoever. It's not realistic to think that way. It's too extreme. You're putting one thing down at the lower extreme and the other way up at the upper. In Buddhism, we call that kind of mind dualistic.

Furthermore, if humans are completely negative by nature, what is the point of seeking a higher idea? Anyway, ideas are not realizations. People always want to know all about the highest attainments or the nature of God, but such intellectual knowledge has nothing to do with their lives or their minds. True religion should be the pursuit of self-realization, not an exercise in the accumulation of facts.

In Buddhism, we are not particularly interested in the quest for intellectual knowledge alone. We are much more interested in understanding what's happening here and now, in comprehending our present experiences, what we are at this very moment, our fundamental nature. We want to know how to find satisfaction, how to find happiness and joy instead of depression and misery, how to overcome the feeling that our nature is totally negative.

Lord Buddha himself taught that basically, human nature is pure, egoless, just as the sky is by nature clear, not cloudy. Clouds come and go, but the blue sky is always there; clouds don't alter the fundamental nature of the sky. Similarly, the human mind is fundamentally pure, not one with the ego. Anyway, whether you are a religious person or not, if you can't separate yourself from your ego, you're completely misguided; you've created for yourself a totally unrealistic philosophy of life that has nothing whatsoever to do with reality.

Instead of grasping at intellectual knowledge, wanting to know what's the highest thing going, you'd be much better off trying to gain an understanding of the basic nature of your own mind and how to deal with it right now. It is so important to know how to act effectively: method is the key to any religion, the most important thing to learn.

Say you hear about an amazing treasure house containing jewels for the taking but don't have the key to the door: all your fantasies about how you'll spend your new-found wealth are a complete hallucination. Similarly, fantasizing about wonderful religious ideas and peak experiences but having no interest in immediate action or the methods of attainment is totally unrealistic. If you have no method, no key, no way to bring your religion into your everyday life, you'd be better off with Coca-Cola. At least that quenches your thirst. If your religion is simply an idea, it's as insubstantial as air. You should be very careful that you understand exactly what religion is and how it should be practiced.

Lord Buddha himself said, "Belief is not important. Don't believe what I say just because I said it." These were his dying words. "I have taught many different methods because there are many different individuals. Before you embrace any of them, use your wisdom to check that they fit your psychological make-up, your own mind. If my methods seem to make sense and work for you, by all means adopt them. But if you don't relate to them, even though they might sound wonderful, leave them be. They were taught for somebody else."

These days, you can't tell most people that they should believe something just because Buddha said, because God said. It's not enough for them. They'll reject it; they want proof. But those who cannot understand that the nature of their mind is pure will be unable to see the possibility of discovering their innate purity and will lose whatever chance they had to do so. If you think that your mind is fundamentally negative, you tend to lose all hope.

Of course, the human mind has both positive and negative sides. But the negative is transient, very temporary. Your up and down emotions are like clouds in the sky; beyond them, the real, basic human nature is clear and pure.

Many people misunderstand Buddhism. Even some professors of Buddhist studies look at just the words and interpret what the Buddha taught very literally. They don't understand his methods, which are the real essence of his teachings. In my opinion, the most important aspect of any religion is its methods: how to put that religion into your own experience. The better you understand how to do that, the more effective your religion becomes. Your practice becomes so natural, so realistic; you easily come to understand your own nature, your own mind, and you don't get surprised by whatever you find in it. Then, when you understand the nature of your own mind, you'll be able to control it naturally; you won't have to push so hard; understanding naturally brings control.

Many people will imagine that control of the mind is some kind of tight, restrictive bondage. Actually, control is a natural state. But you're not going to say that, are you? You're going to say that the mind is uncontrolled by nature, that it is natural for the mind to be uncontrolled. But it's not. When you realize the nature of your uncontrolled mind, control comes as naturally as your present uncontrolled state arises. Moreover, the only way to gain control over your mind is to understand its nature. You can never force your mind, your internal world, to change. Nor can you purify your mind by punishing yourself physically, by beating your body. That's totally impossible. Impurity, sin, negativity or whatever else you want to call it is psychological, a mental phenomenon, so you can't stop it physically. Purification requires a skillful combination of method and wisdom.

To purify your mind, you don't have to believe in something special up there—God, or Buddha. Don't worry about that. When you truly realize the up and down nature of your everyday life, the characteristic nature of your own mental attitude, you'll automatically want to implement a solution.

These days, many people are disillusioned with religion; they seem to think it doesn't work. Religion works. It offers fantastic solutions to all your problems. The problem is that people don't understand the characteristic nature of religion, so they don't have the will to implement its methods.

Consider the materialistic life. It's a state of complete agitation and conflict. You can never fix things to be the way you want. You can't just wake up in the morning and decide exactly how you want your day to unfold. Forget about weeks, months, or years; you can't even predetermine one day. If I were to ask you right now if you can get up in the morning and set exactly how your day was going to go, how you were going to feel each moment, what would you say? There's no way you can do that, is there?

No matter how much you make yourself materially comfortable, no matter how you arrange your house—you have this, you have that; you put one thing here, you put another there—you can never manipulate your mind in the same way. You can never determine the way you're going to feel all day. How can you fix your mind like that? How can you say, "Today I'm going to be like this"? I can tell you with absolute certainty, as long as your mind is uncontrolled, agitated and dualistic, there's no way; it's impossible. When I say this, I'm not putting you down; I'm just talking about the way the mind works.

What all this goes to show is that no matter how you make yourself materially comfortable, no matter how much you tell yourself, "Oh, this makes me happy, today I'm going to be happy all day long," it's impossible to predetermine your life like that. Automatically, your feelings keep changing, changing, changing. This shows that the materialistic life doesn't work. However, I don't mean that you should renounce the worldly life and become ascetics. That's not what I'm saying. My point is that if you understand spiritual principles correctly and act accordingly, you will find much greater satisfaction and meaning in your life than you will by relying on the sense world alone. The sense world alone cannot satisfy the human mind.

Thus, the only purpose for the existence of what we call religion is for us to understand the nature of our own psyche, our own mind, our own feelings. Whatever name we give to our spiritual path, the most important thing is that we get to know our own experiences, our own feelings. Therefore, the lamas' experience of Buddhism is that instead of emphasizing belief, it places prime importance on personal experimentation, putting Dharma methods into action and assessing the effect they have on our minds: do these methods help? Have our minds changed or are they just as uncontrolled as they ever were? This is Buddhism, and this method of checking the mind is called meditation.

It's an individual thing; you can't generalize. It all comes down to personal understanding, personal experience. If your path is not providing solutions to your problems, answers to your questions, satisfaction to your mind, you must check up. Perhaps there's something wrong with your point of view, your understanding. You can't necessarily conclude that there's something wrong with your religion just because you tried it and it didn't work. Different individuals have their own ideas, views, and understanding of religion, and can make mistakes. Therefore, make sure that the way you understand your religion's ideas and methods is correct. If you make the right effort on the basis of right understanding, you will experience deep inner satisfaction. Thus, you'll prove to yourself that satisfaction does not depend on anything external. True satisfaction comes from the mind.

We often feel miserable and our world seems upside-down because we believe that external things will work exactly as we plan and expect them to. We expect things that are changeable by nature not to change, impermanent things to last forever. Then, when they do change, we get upset. Getting upset when something in your house breaks shows that you didn't really understand its impermanent nature. When it's time for something to break, it's going to break, no matter what you expect.

Nevertheless, we still expect material things to last. Nothing material lasts; it's impossible. Therefore, to find lasting satisfaction, you should put more effort into your spiritual practice and meditation than into manipulating the world around you. Lasting satisfaction comes from your mind, from within you. Your main problem is your uncontrolled, dissatisfied mind, whose nature is suffering.

Knowing this, when any problem arises, instead of getting upset because of your unfulfilled expectations and busily distracting yourself with some external activity, relax, sit down and examine the situation with your own mind. That is a much more constructive way of dealing with problems and pacifying your mind. Moreover, when you do this, you are allowing your innate knowledge-wisdom to grow. Wisdom can never grow in an agitated, confused and restless mind.

Agitated mental states are a major obstacle to your gaining of wisdom. So too is the misconception that your ego and your mind's nature are one and the same. If that's what you believe, you'll never be able to separate them and reach beyond ego. As long as you believe that you are totally in the nature of sin and negativity you will never be able to transcend them. What you believe is very important and very effectively perpetuates your wrong views. In the West, people seem to think that if you aren't one with your ego, you can't have a life, get a job or do anything. That's a dangerous delusion—you can't separate ego from mind, ego from life. That's your big problem. You think that if you lose your ego you'll lose your personality, your mind, your human nature.

That's simply not true; you shouldn't worry about that. If you lose your ego you'll be happy—you *should* be happy. But of course, this raises the question, what is the ego? In the West, people seem to have so many words for the ego, but do they know what the ego really is? Anyway, it doesn't matter how perfect your English is, the ego is not a word; the word is just a symbol. The actual ego is within you: it's the wrong conception that your self is independent, permanent and inherently existent. In reality, what you believe to be "I" doesn't exist.

If I were to ask everybody here to check deeply, beyond words, what they thought the ego was, each person would have a different idea. I'm not joking; this is my experience. You should check your own. We always say, very superficially,

"That's your ego," but we have no idea of what the ego really is. Sometimes we even use the term pejoratively: "Oh, don't worry, that's just your ego," or something like that, but if you check up more deeply, you'll see that the average person thinks that the ego is his personality, his life. Men feel that if they were to lose their ego, they'd lose their personalities, they'd no longer be men; women feel that were they to lose their ego they'd lose their female qualities. That's not true; not true at all. Still, based on Westerners' interpretation of life and ego, that's pretty much what it comes down to. They think the ego is something positive in the sense that it's essential for living in society; that if you don't have an ego, you can't mix in society. You check up more deeply—on the mental level, not the physical. It's interesting.

Even many psychologists describe the ego at such a superficial level that you'd think it was a physical entity. From the Buddhist point of view, the ego is a mental concept, not a physical thing. Of course, symptoms of ego activity can manifest externally, such as when, for example, someone's angry and his face and body reflect that angry vibration. But that's not anger itself; it's a symptom of anger. Similarly, ego is not its external manifestations but a mental factor, a psychological attitude. You can't see it from the outside.

When you meditate, you can see why today you're up, tomorrow you're down: mood swings are caused by your mind. People who don't check within themselves come up with very superficial reasons like, "I'm unhappy today because the sun's not shining," but most of the time your ups and downs are due to primarily psychological factors.

When a strong wind blows, the clouds vanish and blue sky appears. Similarly, when the powerful wisdom that understands the nature of the mind arises, the dark clouds of ego disappear. Beyond the ego—the agitated, uncontrolled mind—lie everlasting peace and satisfaction. That's why Lord Buddha prescribed penetrative analysis of both your positive and your negative sides. In particular, when your negative mind arises, instead of being afraid, you should examine it more closely.

You see, Buddhism is not at all a tactful religion, always trying to avoid giving offense. Buddhism addresses precisely what you are and what your mind is doing in the here and now.

That's what makes it so interesting. You can't expect to hear only positive things. Sure you have a positive side, but what about the negative aspects of your nature? To gain an equal understanding of both, an understanding of the totality of your being, you have to look at your negative characteristics as well as the positive ones, and not try to cover them up.

I don't have much more to say right now, but I'd be happy to try to answer some questions.

Q. Lama, were you saying that we should express rather than suppress our negative actions, that we should let the negativity come out?

Lama. It depends. There are two things. If the negative emotion has already bubbled to the surface, it's probably better to express it in some way, but it's preferable if you can deal with it before it has reached that level. Of course, if you don't have a method of dealing with strong negative emotions and you try to bottle them up deep inside, eventually that can lead to serious problems, such as an explosion of anger that causes someone to pick up a gun and shoot people. What Buddhism teaches is a method of examining that emotion with wisdom and digesting it through meditation, which allows the emotion to simply dissolve. Expressing strong negative emotions externally leaves a tremendously deep impression on your consciousness. This kind of imprint makes it easier for you to react in the same harmful way again, except that the second time it may be even more powerful than the first. This sets up a karmic chain of cause and effect that perpetuates such negative behavior. Therefore, you have to exercise skill and judgment in dealing with negative energy, learn when and how to express it and, especially, know how to recognize it early in the piece and digest it with wisdom.

Q. Could you please explain the relationship between Buddhist meditation techniques and hatha yoga?

Lama. In Buddhism we tend to focus more on penetrative introspection than on bodily movement, although there are certain practices where the meditation techniques are enhanced by physical exercises. In general, Buddhist meditation teaches us to look within at what we are, to understand our own true nature. All the same, Buddhist meditation does not necessarily imply sitting in the lotus position with your eyes closed—meditation can be brought into every aspect of your daily life. It is important to be aware of everything you do so that you don't unconsciously harm either yourself or others. Whether you are walking, talking, working, eating...whatever you do, be conscious of the actions of your body, speech and mind.

Q. Do Buddhists control their *prana* [wind energy] completely through the mind?
Lama. Yes. If you can control your mind, you can control anything. It's impossible to control your physical body without first controlling your mind. If you try to control your body forcibly, if you pump yourself up with no understanding of the mind-body relationship, it can be very dangerous and cause your mind great harm.

Q. Can you reach as deep a state of meditation through walking as you can through sitting?
Lama. Sure, it's theoretically possible, but it depends upon the individual. For beginners, it is obviously much easier to attain deeper states of concentration through sitting meditation. Experienced meditators, however, can maintain single-pointed concentration, a fully integrated mind, whatever they're doing, including walking. Of course, if someone's mind is completely disturbed, even sitting meditation may not be enough for him to integrate his mind. One of the hallmarks of Buddhism is that you can't say that everybody should do this, everybody should be like that; it depends on the individual. However, we do have a clearly defined, step-like path of meditation practice: first you develop this, then you move on to that, and so on through the various levels of concentration. Similarly, the entire path to enlightenment—we call it the *lam-rim*— has been laid out in a graded, logical fashion so that each person can find his or her own level and take it from there.

Q. Lama, can the various negative thoughts that arise in our minds come from a source outside of ourselves, from other people, or perhaps from spirits?
Lama. Well, that's a very good question. The real source, the deep root of negativity, lies within our own minds, but for this to manifest usually requires interaction with a cooperative, environmental cause, such as other people or the material

31

world. For example, some people experience mood swings as a result of astrological influences, such as the vibration of planetary movement. Others' emotions fluctuate because of hormonal changes in their bodies. Such experiences do not come from their minds alone but through the interaction of physical and mental energy. Of course, we would also say that the fact that we find ourselves in a body susceptible to this kind of change originally comes from our minds. But I don't think Lord Buddha would say that there is some outer spirit harming you like that. What is possible is that your inner energy is relating to some outer energy, and that it is that interaction that makes you sick.

You can see from your own life experiences how the environment can affect you. When you're amongst peaceful, generous, happy people, you're inclined to feel happy and peaceful yourself. When you're amongst angry, aggressive people, you tend to become like them. The human mind is like a mirror. A mirror does not discriminate but simply reflects whatever's before it, no matter whether it's horrible or wonderful. Similarly, your mind takes on the aspect of your surroundings, and if you're not aware of what's going on, your mind can fill with garbage. Therefore, it is very important to be conscious of your surroundings and how they affect your mind.

The thing that you have to understand about religion is how your religion relates to your own mind, how it relates to the life you lead. If you can manage that, religion is fantastic; the realizations are there. You don't need to emphasize belief in God, or Buddha, or sin or whatever; don't worry about all that. Just act out of right understanding as best you can and you'll get results, even today. Forget about super consciousness or super universal love—universal love grows slowly, steadily, gradually. If, however, you're just clinging to the notion, "Oh, fantastic! Infinite knowledge, infinite power," you're simply on a power trip. Of course, spiritual power really does exist, but the only way you can get it is by engaging in the proper spiritual actions. Power comes from within you; part of you becomes power, too. Don't think that the only true power is up there, somewhere in the sky. You have power; your mind is power.

Q. Perception is one of the five aggregates that, according to Buddhist philosophy, constitute a person. How does it work?
Lama. Yes, that's another good question. Most of the time, our perception is illusory; we're not perceiving reality. Sure, we see the sense world—attractive shapes, beautiful colors, nice tastes and so forth—but we don't actually perceive the real, true nature of the shapes, colors and tastes we see. That's how most of the time our perception is mistaken. So our mistaken perception processes the information supplied by our five senses and transmits incorrect information to our mind, which reacts under the influence of the ego. The result of all this is that most of the time we are hallucinating, not seeing the true nature of things, not under- standing the reality of even the sense world.

Q. Does past karma affect our perception?
Lama. Yes, of course. Past karma affects our perception a lot. Our ego grasps at our uncontrolled perception's view, and our mind just follows along: that entire uncontrolled situation is what we call karma. Karma is not simply some irrelevant theory; it's the everyday perceptions in which we live, that's all.

Q. Lama, what is the relationship between the body and mind as far as food is concerned.
Lama. Body is not mind, mind is not body, but the two have a very special connection. They are very closely linked, very sensitive to changes in each other. For example, when people take drugs, the substance doesn't affect the mind directly. But since the mind is connected to the body's nervous system and sense organs, changes induced in the nervous system by the drug throw it out of harmony and cause the mind to hallucinate. There's a very strong connection between the body and the mind. In Tibetan tantric yoga, we take advantage of that strong connection: by concentrating strongly on the body's psychic channels we can affect the mind accordingly. Therefore, even in everyday life, the food you eat and the other things your body touches have an effect on your mind.

Q. Is fasting good for you?
Lama. Fasting is not all that important unless you are engaged in certain special mind training practices. Then, fasting may even be essential. This is certainly the lamas' experience. For

example, if you eat and drink all day and then try to meditate in the evening, your concentration will be very poor. Therefore, when we're doing serious meditation, we eat only once a day. In the morning, we just drink tea; at midday we have lunch; and in the evening, instead of eating, we again drink tea. For us, this kind of routine makes life desirably simple and the body very comfortable; but for someone not engaged in mind training, it would probably feel like torture. Normally, we don't advocate fasting. We tell people not to punish themselves but simply to be happy and reasonable and to keep their bodies as healthy as they can. If your body gets weak, your mind becomes useless. When your mind becomes useless, your precious human life becomes useless. But on special occasions, when fasting enhances your meditation practice, when there's a higher purpose, I would say yes, fasting can be good for you.

Thank you very much. If there are no further questions, I won't keep you any longer. Thank you very much.

Brisbane, Australia
28 April 1975

A Glimpse of Buddhist Psychology

The study of Buddhism is not a dry, intellectual undertaking or the skeptical analysis of some religious, philosophical doctrine. On the contrary, when you study Dharma and learn how to meditate, *you* are the main topic; you are mainly interested in your own mind, your own true nature.

Buddhism is a method for controlling the undisciplined mind in order to lead it from suffering to happiness. At the moment, we all have an undisciplined mind, but if we can develop a correct understanding of its characteristic nature, control will follow naturally and we'll be able to release emotional ignorance and the suffering it brings automatically. Therefore, no matter whether you are a believer or a non-believer, religious or not religious, a Christian, a Hindu, or a scientist, black or white, an Easterner or a Westerner, the most important thing to know is your own mind and how it works.

If you don't know your own mind, your misconceptions will prevent you from seeing reality. Even though you might say you're a practitioner of this or that religion, if you investigate more deeply, you might find that you are nowhere. Be careful. No religion is against your knowing your own nature, but all too frequently religious people involve themselves too much in their religion's history, philosophy or doctrine and ignore how and what they themselves are, their present state of being. Instead of using their religion to attain its goals—salvation, liberation, inner freedom, eternal happiness and joy—they play intellectual games with their religion, as if it were a material possession.

Without understanding how your inner nature evolves, how can you possibly discover eternal happiness? Where is eternal happiness? It's not in the sky or in the jungle; you won't find it in the air or under the ground. Everlasting happiness is within you, within your psyche, your consciousness, your mind. That's why it is so important that you investigate the nature of your own mind.

If the religious theory that you learn does not serve to bring happiness and joy into your everyday life, what's the point? Even though you say, "I'm a practitioner of this or that religion," check what you've done, how you've acted, and what you've discovered since you've been following it. And don't be afraid to question yourself in detail. Your own experience is good. It is essential to question everything you do, otherwise, how do you know what you're doing? As I'm sure you know already, blind faith in any religion can never solve your problems.

Many people are lackadaisical about their spiritual practice. "It's easy. I go to church every week. That's enough for me." That's not the answer. What's the purpose of your religion? Are you getting the answers you need or is your practice simply a joke? You have to check. I'm not putting anybody down, but you have to be sure of what you're doing. Is your practice perverted, polluted by hallucination, or is it realistic? If your path teaches you to act and exert yourself correctly and leads to spiritual realizations such as love, compassion and wisdom, then obviously it's worthwhile. Otherwise, you're just wasting your time.

The mental pollution of misconceptions is far more dangerous than drugs. Wrong ideas and faulty practice get deeply rooted in your mind, build up during your life, and accompany your mind into the next one. That is much more dangerous than some physical substance.

All of us, the religious and the non-religious, Easterner and Westerner alike, want to be happy. Everybody seeks happiness, but are you looking in the right place? Perhaps happiness is *here* but you're looking *there*. Make sure you seek happiness where it can be found.

We consider Lord Buddha's teaching to be more akin to psychology and philosophy than to what you might usually imagine religion to be. Many people seem to think that religion is mostly a question of belief, but if your religious practice relies mainly on faith, sometimes one skeptical question from a friend—

"What on earth are you doing?"—can shatter it completely: "Oh my god! Everything I've been doing is wrong." Therefore, before you commit yourself to any spiritual path, make sure you know exactly what you're doing.

Buddhist psychology teaches that emotional attachment to the sense world results from physical and mental feelings. Your five senses provide information to your mind, producing various feelings, all of which can be classified into three groups: pleasant, unpleasant and neutral. These feelings arise in response to either physical or mental stimuli.

When we experience pleasant feelings, emotional attachment ensues, and when that pleasant feeling subsides, craving arises, the desire to experience it again. The nature of this mind is dissatisfaction; it disturbs our mental peace because its nature is agitation. When we experience unpleasant feelings, we automatically dislike and want to get rid of them; aversion arises, again disturbing our mental peace. When we feel neutral, we ignore what's going on and don't want to see reality. Thus, whatever feelings arise in our daily lives— pleasant, unpleasant or neutral—they disturb us emotionally and there's no balance or equanimity in our minds.

So, examining your own feelings in this way has nothing to do with belief, has it? This is not some Eastern, Himalayan mountain thing. This is you; this is your thing. You can't refute what I'm saying by claiming, "I have no feelings." It's so simple, isn't it?

Furthermore, many of our negative actions are reactions to feeling. See for yourself. When you feel pleasant as a result of contact with people or other sense objects, analyze exactly how you feel, why you feel pleasant. The pleasant feeling is not in the external object, is it? It's in your mind. I'm sure we can all agree that the pleasant feeling is not outside of you. So, why do you feel that way? If you experiment like this, you will discover that happiness and joy, discomfort and unhappiness, and neutral feelings are all within you. You will find that you yourself are mainly responsible for the feelings you experience and that you cannot blame others for the way you feel: "He makes me miserable; she makes me miserable; that stuff makes me miserable." You cannot blame society for your problems, although that's what we always do, isn't it? It's not realistic.

Once you realize the true evolution of your mental problems, you'll never blame any other living being for how you feel. That realization is the beginning of good communication with and respect for others. Normally, we're unconscious; we act unconsciously and automatically disrespect and hurt others. We don't care; we just do it, that's all.

Many people, even some psychologists, seem to think that you can stop the emotion of craving-desire by feeding it with some object or other: if you're suffering because your husband or wife has left you, getting another one will solve your problem. That's impossible. Without understanding the characteristic nature of your feelings of pleasant, unpleasant and neutral, you will never discover the nature of your mental attitudes, and without discovering that, you can never put an end to your emotional problems.

For instance, Buddhism says you should feel compassion and love for all living beings. How can you possibly feel even equanimity for all beings while the ignorant, dualistic mind is functioning so strongly within you? You can't, because emotionally you are too extreme. When you feel happy because a pleasant feeling has arisen through contact with a particular object, you grossly exaggerate what you consider to be the good qualities of that object, inflating your emotions as much as you possibly can. But you know that your mind can't stay up like that. It's impermanent, transitory, so of course, you soon crash back down. Then, automatically, your unbalanced mind gets depressed. You have to understand exactly how much energy you expend in pursuit of or in flight from mental feelings. We are always too extreme; we have to find the middle way.

If you look a little deeper, you will also find that feelings are responsible for all the conflict in the world. From two small children fighting over a piece of candy to two huge nations fighting over their very existence, what are they fighting for? For pleasant feelings. Even children too young to speak will fight because they want to feel happy.

Through meditation you can easily see the truth of all this. Meditation reveals everything that's in your mind; all your garbage, all your positivity; everything can be seen through meditation. But don't think that meditation means just sitting on the floor in the lotus position doing nothing. Being conscious, aware of everything that you do—walking, eating, drinking, talking—is meditation. The sooner you realize this, the quicker will you realize that you yourself are responsible for your actions, that you yourself are responsible for the happy feelings you want and the unhappy feelings you don't, and that nobody else controls you.

When a pleasant feeling arises and then, as is its nature, subsides, causing you to feel frustrated because you want it again, that's not created by God, Krishna, Buddha or any other outside entity. Your own actions are responsible. Isn't that easy to see? The weak mind thinks, "Oh, he made me sick, she makes me feel horrible." That's the weak mind at work, always trying to blame somebody or something else. Actually, I think that examining your everyday life experiences to see how your physical and mental feelings arise is a wonderful thing to do. You're learning all the time; there's no such time that you're not learning. In that way, through the application of your own knowledge-wisdom, you will discover that the realization of everlasting peace and joy is within you. Unfortunately, the weak mind doesn't possess much knowledge-wisdom energy; you have to nurture that energy within your own mind.

Why does Mahayana Buddhism teach us to develop a feeling of equanimity for all sentient beings? We often choose just one small thing, one small atom, one single living being, thinking, "This is the one for me; this is the best." Thus, we create extremes of value: we grossly exaggerate the value of the one we like and engender disdain for all the rest. This is not good for you, for your mental peace. Instead, you should examine your behavior, "Why am I doing this? My unrealistic, egocentric mind is polluting my consciousness." Then, by meditating on equanimity—all sentient beings are exactly the same in wanting happiness and not desiring suffering—you can learn to eliminate the extremes of tremendous attachment to one and tremendous aversion to the other. In this way you can easily keep your mind balanced and healthy. Many people have had this experience.

Therefore, Lord Buddha's psychology can be of great help when you're trying to deal with the frustrations that disturb your daily life. Remember that when pleasant feelings arise, desire, craving and attachment follow in their wake; when unpleasant feelings arise, aversion and hatred appear; and when you feel neutral, ignorance, blindness to reality, occupies your mind. If, through these teachings, you can learn the reality of how your feelings arise and how you react to them, your life will be much improved and you will experience much happiness, peace and joy.

Are there any questions?

Q. Buddhism always talks about karma. What is it?
Lama. Karma is your experiences of body and mind. The word itself is Sanskrit; it means cause and effect. Your experiences of mental and physical happiness or unhappiness are the effects of certain causes, but those effects themselves become the cause of future results. One action produces a reaction; that is karma. Both Eastern philosophies and science explain that all matter is inter-related; if you can understand that, you will understand how karma works. All existence, internal and external, does not come about accidentally; the energy of all internal and external phenomena is interdependent. For example, your body's energy is related to the energy of your parents' bodies; their bodies' energy is related to their parents' bodies, and so forth. That sort of evolution is karma.

Q. What is *nirvana* and do many people attain it?
Lama. When you develop your powers of concentration such that you can integrate your mind into single-pointed concentration, you will gradually diminish your ego's emotional reactions until they disappear altogether. At that point, you transcend your ego and discover an everlasting, blissful, peaceful state of mind. That is what we call nirvana. Many people have attained this state and many more are well on their way to it.

Q. In nirvana, do you cease to exist in a bodily form; does the person disappear?
Lama. No, you still have a form, but it doesn't have an uncontrolled nervous system like the one we have now. And don't worry, when you attain nirvana you still exist, but in a state of perfect happiness. So, try hard to reach it as soon as possible.

Q. Didn't Buddha say that he would never be reborn once he had attained nirvana?

Lama. Perhaps, but what did he mean? He meant that he would not take an uncontrolled rebirth impelled by the energy force of ego, which is the way we samsaric sentient beings are reborn. Instead, he can reincarnate with perfect control, his only purpose being to help mother sentient beings.

Q. You spoke a lot about pleasure and happiness, and I am trying to get clear in my mind the distinction between the two. Are they the same? Can one become attached to pleasure but not to happiness?
Lama. They're the same thing and we get attached to both. What we should aim for is the experience of pleasure without attachment; we should enjoy our feelings of happiness while understanding the nature of the subject, our mind, the object, and our feelings. Someone who has reached nirvana is able to do this.

Q. I would like to clarify the Buddhist meaning of meditation. Am I right in interpreting it as "observing the passage of your mind"?
Lama. Yes, you can think of it that way. As I said before, Buddhist meditation doesn't necessarily mean sitting cross-legged with your eyes closed. Simply observing how your mind is responding to the sense world as you go about your business—walking, talking, shopping, whatever—can be a really perfect meditation and bring a perfect result.

Q. With respect to rebirth, what is it that is reborn?
Lama. When you die, your consciousness separates from your body, enters the intermediate state, and from there it is born into another physical form. We call that rebirth. Physical and mental energy are different from each other. Physical energy is extremely limited, but mental energy always has continuity.

Q. Is it possible for the consciousness to develop in the after-death state or is it only in life that consciousness can evolve?
Lama. During the death process, your consciousness keeps flowing, just like electricity, which comes from the generator but flows continually through different houses, different appliances and so forth, occupying different things. So, it is possible for the consciousness to develop in the intermediate state.

41

Q. So the mind does not need a physical body to develop?
Lama. Well, there is an intermediate state body, but it's not like ours; it's a very light, psychic body.

Q. When you recite mantras, do you ever concentrate on any of the body's physical organs or do you focus only on your mind? Can you concentrate on your *chakras,* or energy centers?
Lama. It's possible, but you have to remember that there are different methods for different purposes. Don't think that Lord Buddha taught only one thing. Buddhism contains thousands upon thousands, perhaps even countless, methods of meditation, all given in order to suit the varying propensities and dispositions of the infinite individual living beings.

Q. Is the consciousness that develops during our life and leaves when we die a part of some supreme consciousness? Like God or universal consciousness?
Lama. No, it's a very ordinary, simple mind and is in direct continuity with the mind you have right now. The difference is that it has separated from your body and is seeking another. This intermediate state mind is under the control of karma, and is agitated, conflicted and confused. There's no way you can call it higher or supreme.

Q. Are you familiar with the Hindu concepts of *atman* and *brahman?*
Lama. While Hindu philosophy accepts the idea of a soul [atman], Buddhism does not. We completely deny the existence of a self-existent I, or a permanent, independent soul. Every aspect of your body and mind is impermanent: changing, changing, changing.... Buddhists also deny the existence of a permanent hell. Every pain, every pleasure we experience is in a state of constant flux; so transitory, so impermanent, always changing, never lasting. Therefore, recognizing the dissatisfactory nature of our existence and renouncing the world in which transitory sense objects contact transitory sense organs to produce transitory feelings, none of which are worth grasping at, we seek instead the everlasting, eternally joyful realizations of enlightenment or nirvana.

Q. Do you think ritual is as important to the Western person trying to practice Buddhism as it is to the Easterner, who has a feeling for it?

Lama. It depends on what you mean. Actual Buddhist meditation doesn't require you to accompany it with material objects; the only thing that matters is your mind. You don't need to ring bells or wave things about. Is that what you mean by ritual? [Yes.] Good; so, you don't need to worry, and that applies equally to the East as it does to the West. Nevertheless, some people do need these things; different minds need different methods. For example, you wear glasses. They're not the most important thing, but some people need them. For the same reason, the various world religions teach various paths according to the individual abilities and levels of their many and varied followers. Therefore, we cannot say, "This is the one true way. Everybody should follow my path."

Q. Are new methods of practice required in the West today?
Lama. No. No new methods are required. All the methods are there already, you just need to discover them.

Q. I am trying to understand the relationship in Buddhism between the mind and the body. Is mind more important than body? For example, in the case of tantric monks who do overtone chanting, obviously they develop a part of their body in order to sing, so just how important is the body?
Lama. The mind is the most important thing, but there are some meditation practices that are enhanced by certain physical yoga exercises. Conversely, if your body is sick, that can affect your mind. So, it's also important to keep your body healthy. But if you concern yourself with only the physical and neglect to investigate the reality of your own mind, that's not wise either; it's unbalanced, not realistic. So, I think we all agree that the mind is more important than the body, but at the same time, we cannot forget about the body altogether. I've seen Westerners come to the East for teachings, and when they hear about Tibetan yogis living in the high mountains without food they think, "Oh, fantastic! I want to be just like Milarepa." That's a mistake. If you were born in the West, your body is used to certain specific conditions, so to keep it healthy, you need to create a conducive environment. You can't do a Himalayan trip. Be wise, not extreme.

Q. Is it true that when a human is born his or her mind is pure and innocent?

Lama. As we all know, when you are born, your mind is not too occupied by intellectual complications. But as you get older and start to think, it begins to fill up with so much information, philosophy, that-this, this is good, that is bad, I should have this, I shouldn't have that…you intellectualize too much, filling your mind with garbage. That certainly makes your mind much worse. Still, that doesn't mean that you were born absolutely pure and that only after the arrival of the intellect did you become negative. It doesn't mean that. Why not? Because if you were fundamentally free of ignorance and attachment, any garbage coming at you would not be able to get in. Unfortunately, we're not like that. Fundamentally, not only are we wide open to whatever intellectual garbage comes our way, but we've got a big welcome sign out. So moment by moment, more and more garbage is piling up in our minds. Therefore, you can't say that children are born with absolutely pure minds. It's wrong. Babies cry because they have feelings. When an unpleasant feeling arises—perhaps they're craving their mother's milk—they cry.

Q. We have this idea of consciousness transmigrating from body to body, from life to life, but if there is continuity of consciousness, why is it that we don't remember our previous lives?

Lama. Too much supermarket information crowding into our minds makes us forget our previous experiences. Even science says that the brain is limited such that new information suppresses the old. They say that, but it's not quite right. What actually happens is that basically, the human mind is mostly unconscious, ignorant, and gets so preoccupied with new experiences that it forgets the old ones. Review the past month: exactly what happened, precisely what feelings did you have, every day? You can't remember, can you? So checking back further, all the way back to the time when you were just a few cells in your mother's womb, then even farther back than that: it's very difficult, isn't it? But if you practice this slowly, slowly, continuously checking within your mind, eventually you'll be able to remember more and more of your previous experiences.

Many of us may have had the experience of reacting very strangely to something that has happened and being perplexed by our reaction, which seems not to have been based on any of this life's experiences: "That's weird. Why did I react like that? I've no idea where that came from." That's because it's based on a previous life's experience. Modern psychologists cannot explain such reactions because they don't understand mental continuity, the beginningless nature of each individual's mind. They don't understand that mental reactions can result from impulses that were generated thousands and thousands of years ago. But if you keep investigating your mind through meditation, you will eventually understand all this through your own experience.

Q. Could it be negative to find out about previous lives? Could it be disturbing?
Lama. Well, it could be either a positive or a negative experience. If you *realize* your previous lives, it will be a positive experience. Disturbance comes from ignorance. You should try to realize the characteristic nature of negativity. When you do, the problem's solved. Understanding the nature of negativity stops the problems it brings. Therefore, right understanding is the only solution to both physical and mental problems. You should always check very carefully how you're expending your energy: will it make you happy or not. That's a big responsibility, don't you think? It's your choice: the path of wisdom or the path of ignorance.

Q. What is the meaning of suffering?
Lama. Mental agitation is suffering; dissatisfaction is suffering. Actually, it is very important to understand the various subtle levels of suffering, otherwise people are going to say, "Why does Buddhism say everybody's suffering? I'm happy." When Lord Buddha talked about suffering, he didn't mean just the pain of a wound or the kind of mental anguish that we often experience. We say that we're happy, but if we check our happiness more closely, we'll find that there's still plenty of dissatisfaction in our minds. From the Buddhist point of view, simply the fact that we can't control our minds is mental suffering; in fact, that's worse than the various physical sufferings we experience. Therefore, when Buddhism talks

about suffering, it's emphasizing the mental level much more than the physical, and that's why, in practical terms, Buddhist teachings are basically applied psychology. Buddhism teaches the nature of suffering at the mental level and the methods for its eradication.

Q. Why do we all experience suffering and what do we learn from it?

Lama. That's so simple, isn't it? Why are you suffering? Because you're too involved in acting out of ignorance and grasping with attachment. You learn from suffering by realizing where it comes from and exactly what it is that makes you suffer. In our infinite previous lives we have had so many experiences but we still haven't learned that much. Many people think that they're learning from their experiences, but they're not. There are infinite past experiences in their unconscious but they still know nothing about their own true nature.

Q. Why do we have the opportunity to be attached?

Lama. Because we're hallucinating; we're not seeing the reality of either the subject or the object. When you understand the nature of an object of attachment, the subjective mind of attachment automatically disappears. It's the foggy mind, the mind that's attracted to an object and paints a distorted projection onto it, that makes you suffer. That's all. It's really quite simple.

Q. I've seen Tibetan images of wrathful deities, but although they were fierce-looking, they didn't look evil. That made me wonder whether or not Buddhism emphasizes evil and bad things.

Lama. Buddhism never emphasizes the existence of external evil. Evil is a projection of your mind. If evil exists, it's within you. There's no outside evil to fear. Wrathful deities are emanations of enlightened wisdom and serve to help people who have a lot of uncontrolled anger. In meditation, the angry person transforms his anger into wisdom, which is then visualized as a wrathful deity; thus the energy of his anger is digested by wisdom. Briefly, that's how the method works.

Q. What do you feel about a person killing another person in self-defense? Do you think people have the right to protect themselves, even at the expense of the aggressor's life?

Lama. In most cases of killing in self-defense, it's still done out of uncontrolled anger. You should protect yourself as best you can without killing the other. For example, if you attack me, I'm responsible to protect myself, but without killing you.

Q. If killing me was the only way you could stop me, would you do it?

Lama. Then it would be better that you kill me.

Well, if there are no further questions, I won't keep you any longer. Thank you very much for everything.

Christchurch, New Zealand
14 June 1975

THE LAMA YESHE WISDOM ARCHIVE

The LAMA YESHE WISDOM ARCHIVE (LYWA) is the collected works of Lama Thubten Yeshe and Lama Thubten Zopa Rinpoche. The ARCHIVE was founded in 1996 by Lama Zopa Rinpoche, its spiritual director, to make available in various ways the teachings it contains. Distribution of free booklets of edited teachings is one of the ways.

Lama Yeshe and Lama Zopa Rinpoche began teaching at Kopan Monastery, Nepal, in 1970. Since then, their teachings have been recorded and transcribed. At present the LYWA contains about 5,000 cassette tapes and approximately 40,000 pages of transcribed teachings on computer disk. Some 3,000 tapes, mostly teachings by Lama Zopa Rinpoche, remain to be transcribed. As Rinpoche continues to teach, the number of tapes in the ARCHIVE increases accordingly. Most of the transcripts have been neither checked nor edited.

Here at the LYWA we are making every effort to organize the transcription of that which has not yet been transcribed, to edit that which has not yet been edited, and generally to do the many other tasks detailed opposite. In all this, we need your help. Please contact us for more information:

LAMA YESHE WISDOM ARCHIVE
PO Box 356
Weston, MA 02493, USA
Telephone (781) 899-9587
email nribush@compuserve.com
Web site: www.fpmt.org

Bank information
For transfers from within the USA:

Name of bank: BankBoston
ABA routing number 011000390 BankBoston N. A.
Account: LYWA 546-81495

Transfers from overseas also need either one or both:
S.W.I.F.T. address: FNBB US 33
Telex 4996527 Boston BSN

THE ARCHIVE TRUST

The work of the LAMA YESHE WISDOM ARCHIVE falls into two categories: archiving and dissemination.

ARCHIVING requires managing the audiotapes of teachings by Lama Yeshe and Lama Zopa Rinpoche that have already been collected, collecting tapes of teachings given but not yet sent to the ARCHIVE, and collecting tapes of Lama Zopa's on-going teachings, talks, advice and so forth as he travels the world for the benefit of all. Tapes are then catalogued and stored safely while being kept accessible for further work.

We organize the transcription of tapes, add the transcripts to the already existent database of teachings, manage this database, have transcripts checked and make transcripts available to editors or others doing research on or practicing these teachings.

Other archiving activities include working with videotapes and photographs of the Lamas and investigating the latest means of preserving ARCHIVE materials.

DISSEMINATION involves making the Lamas' teachings available directly or indirectly through various avenues such as booklets for free distribution, regular books for the trade, lightly edited transcripts, floppy disks, audio- and videotapes, and articles in *Mandala* and other magazines, and on the FPMT web site. Irrespective of the method we choose, the teachings require intensive editing to prepare them for distribution.

This is just a summary of what we do. The ARCHIVE was established with virtually no seed funding and has developed solely through the kindness of the many people mentioned at the front of this booklet.

Our further development similarly depends upon the generosity of those who see the benefit and necessity of this work, and we would be extremely grateful for your help.

The ARCHIVE TRUST has been established to facilitate this work and we hereby appeal to you for your kind support. If you would like to make a contribution to help us with any of the above tasks or to sponsor booklets for free distribution, please contact us at our Brookline (Boston) address.

The LAMA YESHE WISDOM ARCHIVE is a 501(c)(3) tax-deductible, non-profit corporation dedicated to the welfare of all sentient beings and totally dependent upon your donations for its continued existence.

Thank you so much for your support.

ENDORSEMENTS

Last November we published a small report on the activities of the LAMA YESHE WISDOM ARCHIVE entitled *LYWA Booklets: What people are saying about them*, in which we quoted much of the unsolicited feedback we have received since we started publishing and distributing booklets free of charge. There are a few of these left, so please let us know if you would like to see one (they contain no teachings, just what some people have said about our work).

But to give you an idea, here are a couple more comments that have come in since that time:

"Thank you for your donation of 70 copies of Lama Yeshe's *Becoming Your Own Therapist*. My senior literature students ate it up. For most, it was their first direct contact with the Dharma, for others it clarified vague understandings. For myself, *Becoming...* and Lama Zopa's *Virtue and Reality* have been miraculous. Sometimes the truth needs to be heard in 83,999 ways before you finally get it. Thanks to Lama Zopa, Lama Yeshe, FPMT and yourself, life has become beautiful again."

—Literature teacher, California, USA

"Congratulations on publishing a very brilliant book [*Virtue and Reality*]. I am sending you some money. If you can spare up to twelve more copies, I'd love to give them to my Dharma friends in our group. This is one of the best expositions on emptiness in print. Plus the first part. The whole thing is completely immediate. Thanks."

—Educator, England

As mentioned on the preceding pages, we rely solely upon donations to maintain the ARCHIVE, get teachings transcribed, and edit, publish and distribute them. Please support our efforts to benefit others in this way.

We would also be grateful for your feedback. Please send us your thoughts on the teachings we make available and your suggestions as to what you would like to see published.

Thank you again.

Acknowledgments (from first printing)

This booklet is the LAMA YESHE WISDOM ARCHIVE's first publication and, in addition to those people thanked previously, there are many others to thank for its appearance as well.

Without the kindness and compassion of our benefactors, the ARCHIVE itself would not exist and this booklet in particular would not have seen the light of day. Merely mentioning your names here is a grossly inadequate way of thanking you for your generosity, but may you be rewarded by a ceaseless flow of ARCHIVE teachings that will lighten the hearts and minds of all who see them, bringing peace and joy into their lives. Thank you all so much for your donations of funds, time and energy— an endless inspiration in our work for the benefit of all sentient beings. Your patience, too, is worthy of respect.

Our major supporters are Drs. Penny Noyce & Leo Liu, Barry & Connie Hershey and the Hershey Family Foundation, Roger & Claire Ash-Wheeler, Mrs. Lily Chang Wu, Dr. Fu Tsung Mao, Prof. Yang Kai Yun, Henry Lau, T. Y. Alexander, Nancy Pan, Claire Atkins, Peter & Nicole Kedge, Salim Lee, Wisdom Books (London), Datuk Tai Tsu Kuang, Mr. Chuah Kok Leng, Mr. Lee Siong Cheong, Ueli Minder, Lynnea Elkind, Claire Ritter, Tan Swee Eng, Ven. Sangye Khadro, and various other friends in Taiwan and elsewhere.

We are also extremely grateful for the help offered by Jack & Trena Cerveri, Pek Chee Hen, Jacalyn Bennett, Steve & Sybil Rosenberg, Cecily Drucker, Lori Cayton, Sander & Sandra Tideman, Sue Bacchus, Lai Hing Chong, Doss McDavid, Thorhalla Bjornsdottir, Jenny Píng, Jack Sonnabaum, Sundra Singam, Dharmawati Brechbuhl, Tan Swee Eng, Ian & Judy Green, Ven. Carol Corradi, Steve Nahaczewski, Chiu Min Lai, Nalanda Monastery, Tom Waggoner, Irene Lim, Margi Haas, Andrea Eugster, Robyn Brentano, Bill Kelley, Tony Simmons, Lynne Sonenberg, Jhampa Shaneman, Atisha Centre, Dr. Don Brown, Bosco Ho, Cat Wilson, Nan Deal, Carol Royce-Wilder, Janice Allen, Arlene Reiss, Candy Campbell, Kim Whitfield, Carleen Gonder, Diana Abrashkin and Anne Parker.

Finally, I would like to offer special thanks to Henry Lau, Datuk Tai Tsu Kuang, Diane Chen, Wah and T. G. Yeoh, Carol Davies and my mother, Beatrice Ribush, for the important roles they have played in helping bring the ARCHIVE to its present stage of development.

Acknowledgements (from second printing)

We are extremely grateful to our friends and supporters who have made it possible to reprint this booklet. The first run of 10,000 went very quickly and we appreciate both the enthusiastic response to its appearance and the tangible offers of help that have resulted in your holding this booklet in your hand.

All those who helped with the first edition, especially our major supporters, were thanked therein (opposite) and we will remain forever in their debt. Here we would also, or again, like to thank Lily Chang Wu, Wang Fu Chen, Claire Atkins, Yeo Chor Seng, Richard Gere, Cecily Drucker, Bodhicitta Foundation and Prof. Yang Kai Yun, Datuk Tai Tsu Kuang, Janet Moore, Tan Swee Eng, Joan Terry, Mike Liu, Pam & Karuna Cayton, Paula de Wijs, Alfred Leyens, Tom & Suzanne Castles, Sander & Sandra Tideman, Wendy van den Heuvel, Maitreya Instituut, Alice Chen, Carol Fields, Roy Gillett, Luke Bailey, Diana Velez, Sundra Singam, Datin Peggy Lim, Catherine Tan, Jan Willis, Richard Farris, Lorraine Greenfield, Nan Deal, Kimball Whitfield, Tom Waggoner, Christine Adkins, Peter Lian, Lynn Wade, Su Hung, Sue Bacchus, Cat Wilson, Tom Begley, Toby Rhodes, Atisha Centre, Rosa Shen, Robyn Brentano & Bill Kelley, Isabelle Johnston, Wah Yeoh, Grace Hoie, Eric Klaft, Jennifer Thiermann, Faith Bach, Vajrasattva Mountain Centre, Tan Sin Wah, Pamela Butler, Charles Wallace, Losang Dragpa Centre, Nina Holzer, James Johns, Wilma Rhoades, Lynne Sonenberg, Wanda Nettl, Lila Weinberg, Diana Abrashkin, Victoria Huckenpahler, Victoria Scott, Veronica Piastuch, Ann Robertson, Patricia Samovar and John Liberty.

We would also like to express our appreciation for the kind help given by our friends in Kuala Lumpur, Malaysia, who facilitated the printing of this booklet there.

THE FOUNDATION FOR THE PRESERVATION OF THE MAHAYANA TRADITION

The Foundation for the Preservation of the Mahayana Tradition (FPMT) is an international organization of Buddhist meditation study and retreat centers, both urban and rural, monasteries, publishing houses, healing centers and other related activities founded in 1975 by Lama Thubten Yeshe and Lama Thubten Zopa Rinpoche. At present, there are more than one hundred FPMT activities in twenty-one countries worldwide.

The FPMT has been established to facilitate the study and practice of Mahayana Buddhism in general, and the Tibetan Gelug tradition, founded in the fifteenth century by the great scholar, yogi and saint, Lama Je Tsong Khapa, in particular, for the benefit of all sentient beings.

Every two months, the Foundation publishes a magazine, *Mandala*, from its International Office in the United States of America. For a sample issue of the magazine or for more information about the organization, please contact:

FPMT
PO Box 800
Soquel, CA 95073, USA
Telephone (408) 476-8435; fax (408) 476-4823
email fpmt@compuserve.com
or check out our web site at www.fpmt.org

Our web site also offers teachings by His Holiness the Dalai Lama, Lama Yeshe, Lama Zopa Rinpoche and many other highly respected teachers in the tradition; details of the FPMT's educational programs; a complete listing of FPMT centers all over the world and in your area; back issues of *Mandala;* and links to FPMT centers on the web, where you will find details of their programs, and to other interesting Buddhist and Tibetan home pages.

WHAT TO DO WITH DHARMA TEACHINGS

The Buddhadharma is the true source of happiness for all sentient beings. Books like this show you how to put the teachings into practice and integrate them into your life, whereby you get the happiness you seek. Therefore, anything containing Dharma teachings or the names of your teachers is more precious than other material objects and should be treated with respect. To avoid creating the karma of not meeting the Dharma again in future lives, please do not put books (or other holy objects) on the floor or underneath other stuff, step over or sit upon them, or use them for mundane purposes such as propping up wobbly tables. They should be kept in a clean, high place, separate from worldly writings, and wrapped in cloth when being carried around. These are but a few considerations.

Should you need to get rid of Dharma materials, they should not be thrown in the rubbish but burned in a special way. Briefly: do not incinerate such materials with other trash, but alone, and as they burn, recite the mantra OM AH HUM. As the smoke rises, visualize that it pervades all of space, carrying the essence of the Dharma to all sentient beings in the six samsaric realms, purifying their minds, alleviating their suffering, and bringing them all happiness, up to and including enlightenment. Some people might find this practice a bit unusual, but it is given according to tradition. Thank you very much.

DEDICATION

Through the merit created by preparing, reading, thinking about and sharing this book with others, may all teachers of the Dharma live long and healthy lives, may the Dharma spread throughout the infinite reaches of space, and may all sentient beings quickly attain enlightenment.

In whichever realm, country, area or place this book may be, may there be no war, drought, famine, disease, injury, disharmony or unhappiness, may there be only great prosperity, may every thing needed be easily obtained, and may all be guided by only perfectly qualified Dharma teachers, enjoy the happiness of Dharma, have only love and compassion for all beings, and only benefit and never harm each other.

LAMA THUBTEN YESHE was born in Tibet in 1935. At the age of six, he entered the great Sera Monastic University, Lhasa, where he studied until 1959, when the Chinese invasion of Tibet forced him into exile in India. Lama Yeshe continued to study and meditate in India until 1967, when, with his chief disciple, Lama Thubten Zopa Rinpoche, he went to Nepal. Two years later he established Kopan Monastery, near Kathmandu, in order to teach Buddhism to Westerners. In 1974, the Lamas began making annual teaching tours to the West, and as a result of these travels a worldwide network of Buddhist teaching and meditation centers—the Foundation for the Preservation of the Mahayana Tradition—began to develop. In 1984, after an intense decade of imparting a wide variety of incredible teachings and establishing one FPMT activity after another, at the age of forty-nine, Lama Yeshe passed away. He was reborn as Ösel Hita Torres in Spain in 1985, recognized as the incarnation of Lama Yeshe by His Holiness the Dalai Lama in 1986, and, as the monk Lama Tenzin Osel Rinpoche, is studying for his *geshe* degree at the reconstituted Sera Monastery in South India. He is fourteen years old. Lama's remarkable story is told in Vicki Mackenzie's book, *Reincarnation: The Boy Lama* (Wisdom Publications, 1996).

Some of Lama Yeshe's teachings have also been published by Wisdom. Books include *Wisdom Energy; Introduction to Tantra; The Tantric Path of Purification;* and (recently) *The Bliss of Inner Fire.* Transcripts in print are *Light of Dharma; Life, Death and After Death;* and *Transference of Consciousness at the Time of Death.* Available through FPMT centers or at www.wisdompubs.org.

Lama Yeshe on videotape: *Introduction to Tantra, The Three Principal Aspects of the Path,* and *Offering Tsok to Heruka Vajrasattva.* Available from the LAMA YESHE WISDOM ARCHIVE.

DR. NICHOLAS RIBUSH, MB, BS, is a graduate of Melbourne University Medical School (1964) who first encountered Buddhism at Kopan Monastery in 1972. Since then he has been a student of Lamas Yeshe and Zopa Rinpoche and a full time worker for the FPMT. He was a monk from 1974 to 1986. He established FPMT archiving and publishing activities at Kopan in 1973, and with Lama Yeshe founded Wisdom Publications in 1975. Between 1981 and 1996 he served as Wisdom's director, editorial director and director of development. Over the years he has edited and published many teachings by Lama Yeshe and Lama Zopa Rinpoche, and established and/or directed several other FPMT activities, including the International Mahayana Institute, Tushita Mahayana Meditation Centre, the Enlightened Experience Celebration, Mahayana Publications, Kurukulla Center for Tibetan Buddhist Studies and now the Lama Yeshe Wisdom Archive. He has been a member of the FPMT board of directors since its inception in 1983.